GET 誠 MAKOTO+

EVERY MONTH AUTOMATICALLY
(and at a discount)

https://www.MakotoPlus.com

You'll get:

Download the Latest Makoto Issue | Weekly Lessons | Reusable TheJapanShop.com Coupon | Monthly Freebies

誠 MAKOTO

e-zine for learners of Japanese

THEJAPANSHOP.COM
VOLUME 5 | ISSUE 55 | September 2022

ご<ruby>購入<rt>こうにゅう</rt></ruby>
ありがとう
ございます。

Thank you so much
for your purchase!

Furigana is the new Ro-maji

When Yumi and I first started publishing Japanese content online, furigana just wasn't possible. Web browsers weren't advanced enough, and so, I added romaji by the tons. I had always believed reliance on romaji can hinder growth, but I didn't see a way around it.

Eventually, adding furigana to web pages became easy, and we gradually removed the romaji and replaced it with furigana.

But furigana, like romaji, can become a crutch. It can make it "unnecessary" for your brain to read the kanji and as a result, you glide past the kanji.

We've occasionally received requests to add the ability to hide furigana, and I'm happy to say, all the furigana on MakotoPlus.com is now hidden by default. All you have to do is mouse over (or tap on mobile) the kanji to see the furigana.

If you are just starting out, seeing naked kanji without furigana can be intimidating, but I promise you it will get better and the extra effort will pay dividends.

Please check out www.MakotoPlus.com and let me know your thoughts.

Thank you!
Clay & Yumi

P.S. The cover says, おにぎりっておいしいね, which means, "Onigiri is delicious, isn't it?" The speaker is an onigiri. I'm not sure if this qualifies for cannibalism.

WHO ARE WE?

Over two decades ago, Clay & Yumi began **TheJapanesePage.com**, one of the Internet's oldest and largest *free* Japanese instructional sites with hundreds of free articles for beginners of Japanese.

They also maintain **TheJapanShop.com**, a webstore specializing in materials to help learners of Japanese.

Have any questions or comments? Contact us at **help@thejapanshop.com**

In this Issue:

- **Laughs, Jokes, Riddles, and Puns**
- **Vocabulary: 口車に乗る**
- **Prefecture Spotlight: Tokyo**
- **Etymology: 君**
- **Anime Phrase of the Day**
- **Haiku : 小林一茶**
- **Kanji Spotlight: 火**
- **Grammar Time! 〜中**
- **Japanese Readers: Disaster Preparedness Day (beginner) + Tezuka Osamu (Intermediate)**

LEVEL Intermediate
JLPT N3

コンビニでファーストフードを頼んだら、「骨なしチキンの

お客様〜!!」と呼ばれた。

なんかすごく悪口を言われたような気がした。

Scan for Recording

After I ordered fast food at a convenience store, (when the order was ready) I was called the "Boneless chicken customer~!!" I felt like I was being insulted.

Vocabulary:

ジョーク a joke

コンビニで at a convenience store [コンビニ (convenience store) + で (at; indicates the location of action)]

ファーストフードを頼んだら after I ordered fast food [ファーストフード (fast food) + を (indicates the direct object of action) + 頼んだら (after (I) ordered; from 頼む (to order); ~ら means "after; when; if... then"; how to form: Verb (casual past) + ら)]

「骨なしチキンのお客様〜!!」 "Boneless chicken customer~!!" [「」 (quotation marks; " ") + 骨 (bone) + なし (without) + チキン (chicken) + の (of; modifier) + お客様 (customer; client; shopper)]

「骨なしチキンのお客様〜!!」と呼ばれた was called the "Boneless chicken customer~!!" [「骨なしチキンのお客様〜!!」 ("Boneless chicken customer~!!") + と (quotation marker) + 呼ばれた (was/were called; plain passive positive past form of 呼ぶ (to call))]

3

Vocabulary Continued

なんか　something like ...; things like ...; someone like ...

すごく　awfully; very; immensely; severely

悪口を言われた　was being called names [plain passive positive past form of 悪口を言う (to insult; to say something insulting about; to bad-mouth; make a derogatory remark; 悪口 (slander; bad-mouthing; abuse; insult; speaking ill (of)) + を (indicates the direct object of action) + 言う (to call; to say))]

ような気がした　felt like [plain past form of ような気がする (have a feeling that; feels like; seems like); how to form: Verb (casual) + ような + 気がする; 「気がする」 is used when you sense something]

VOCABULARY

Learn Useful Words, Phrases, and Sayings

くちぐるま　の
口車に乗る

to fall for someone's line; be cajoled; be taken in by someone's sweet talk

Scan for Recording

ⓘ Use this with people who are easily flattered or easily led to believe the unbelievable.

The use of 乗る for "to be carried away" or "get fooled into joining..." is common in Japanese.

EXAMPLE SENTENCE:

あのおばあさんは、詐欺師の口車に乗って大金をだまし取られてしまった。

That old woman was taken in by a swindler who cajoled her into giving him a lot of money.

Example Sentence

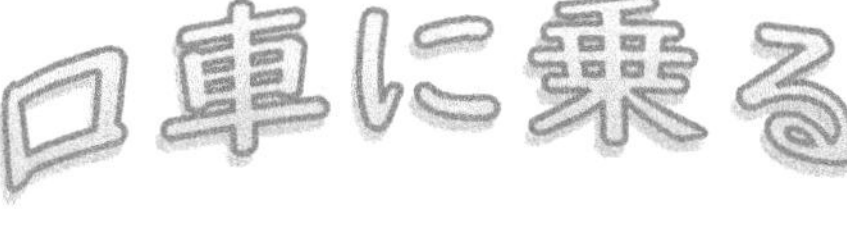

VOCABULARY:

あの　that

おばあさん　old lady [おばあさん can mean "grandmother" or "old lady"]

詐欺師　a swindler; a crook; con-artist [詐欺 (con-artist) ＋ 師 (master)]

5

Vocabulary Continued

口車　cajolery; wheedling [口車 means "mouth wheel" implying a mouth moving fast and smooth to con people before they can think]

乗って　ride and… [*te*-form of 乗る (to ride~); *te*-form conjunctive]

口車に乗って　taken in by; brought into

大金　a large amount of money [大 (big) + 金 (money)]

だまし取られて　got something stolen by deception [*te*-form of だまし取られる which is passive of だまし取る (to steal something by deception); compound word (だます (to deceive) + 取る (to take away))]

だまし取られてしまった　(unfortunately) have taken away by trickery [~てしまった is the plain past form of ~てしまう (refers to a regrettable event or negative meaning); how to form: Verb て-form + しまった]

とうきょう
Tokyo 東京

Japanese: 東京都 *tōkyō to*

Capital: 東京 Tōkyō

Population: 13,988,129 (2022)

DID YOU KNOW?

Tokyo is the capital of Japan and the largest metropolitan area in the world. It is the seat of the Japanese government and where the Imperial Palace is located. Tokyo is made of 23 main city wards and several other cities, towns, and islands. Someone born in Tokyo is known as 江戸っ子 a child of Edo, the old name for Tokyo.

PLACES TO SEE:

- **Tokyo Tower**—Tokyo's iconic 333 meter (1,092) tower. Its design is based on the Eiffel Tower in Paris.

- **Akihabara**—famous for its many electronic and *otaku* shops.

- **Tsukiji Fish Market**—Japan's largest fish market.

- **Tokyo Skytree**—at 634 meters (2,080 feet), it is the tallest building in Japan. Enjoy (or be terrified by) a 360-degree panoramic view of Tokyo from the observation deck.

FAMOUS FOR:

- **Crowds**—with 13 million people, Tokyo is truly a city that never sleeps.

- **Neon Jungle**—of Shibuya and Shinjuku at night.

- **Tokugawa Ieyasu** made Edo (the old name for Tokyo) his base when he became shogun in 1603.

- **Tokyo Imperial Palace**—the main residence of the Emperor of Japan.

- **Vastness**—skyscrapers, crowded subways, and the hustle and bustle of a large metropolis.

- **Regional flavors**—Shibuya for fashionable shopping; Shinjuku for luxury hotels and the seedy Kabukicho; Chiyoda for being the seat of the government as well as having the Imperial Palace; Akihabara for electronics; and many more.

東京

ごげん
語源
ETYMOLOGY

言葉の語源　*kotoba no gogen* – The origin of words:

くん
「君」
"Kun"

Scan for Recording

日本（にほん）では、若（わか）い男性（だんせい）や小（ちい）さい男（おとこ）の子（こ）の名前（なまえ）を「君（くん）」をつけて呼（よ）びます。「まことくん」といった感（かん）じです。ところが、国会（こっかい）で国会議員（こっかいぎいん）や総理大臣（そうりだいじん）も「君（くん）」をつけて呼（よ）びます。岸田文雄君（きしだふみおくん）とか、安倍晋三君（あべしんぞうくん）と言（い）った具合（ぐあい）です。どうして君（くん）をつけるのでしょうか？これは、明治時代（めいじじだい）、江戸時代（えどじだい）の末期（まっき）にさかのぼります。吉田松陰（よしだしょういん）という人（ひと）が始（はじ）めた「松下村塾（しょうかそんじゅく）」でたくさんの若者（わかもの）たちが勉強（べんきょう）していましたが、身分（みぶん）によって名前（なまえ）の呼（よ）び方（かた）が違（ちが）いました。相手（あいて）が武士（ぶし）なら「佐々木様（ささきさま）はどう思（おも）われますか？」という呼（よ）び方（かた）になります

Continued

し、相手が農民なら「佐々木殿の意見を聞きたい。」となります。

身分によって呼び方が違うのはよくないと、吉田松陰はすべての生徒

に「君」を付けて呼ぶことを勧めました。相手の身分に関係なく、

相手を尊重して話ができるからです。これが国会でも取り上げられ

て、今でも続く習慣になりました。

"Kun"

In Japan, young men and small boys are called by their names with "kun". For example, "Makoto-kun". However, members of the National Diet and the prime minister are also addressed with "kun". For example, Kishida Fumio-kun, Abe Shinzou-kun, and so on. Why do we attach "kun"?

It goes back to the Meiji Era (1868-1912) and the end of the Edo Period (1603-1868).

Many young men were studying at the "Shoukason-juku" which was started by a man named Yoshida Shouin, but the way their names were called varied depending on their status. If the person was a samurai, they would say, "What do you think, Sasaki-sama?" If the person was a farmer, they would say, "We would like to hear your opinion, Sasaki-dono." Yoshida Shouin believed that it was not good to address students differently according to their status, so he recommended that all students be addressed with "kun". This is so they could talk to others with respect, regardless of their status. This was taken up even in the Diet and became a custom that still continues to this day.

Vocabulary

語源 etymology; origin of a word

「君」 "kun" [「」 (quotation marks; " ") + 君 (kun; Mr (junior); master; boy)]

日本では in Japan [日本 (Japan) + で (in; indicates the location of action) + は (adds emphasis)]

若い男性や小さい男の子 young men and small boys [若い (young; youthful) + 男性 (man; male) + や (and; such things as …) + 小さい (small; little) + 男の子 (boy; son; young man)]

若い男性や小さい男の子の名前を「君」をつけて呼びます young men and small boys are called by their names with "kun" [若い男性や小さい男の子 (young men and small boys) + の (of; modifier) + 名前 (name) + を (indicates the direct object of action) + 「君」 ("kun") + つけて (て-form of つける (to attach; to join; to add; to append; to affix; to stick) which is used to attach to the next verb 呼びます) + 呼びます (to call)]

「まことくん」といった感じです for example, "Makoto-kun" [「まことくん」 ("Makoto-kun") + といった (like; such as ~; how to form: Noun + といった) + 感じ (sense; feeling; impression) + です (be; is)]

ところが even so; however; still; whereupon; even though

国会で in the National Diet [国会 (National Diet; legislative assembly of Japan) + で (in; of; indicates the location of action)]

国会議員や総理大臣も「君」をつけて呼びます Diet members and the prime minister are also addressed with "kun" [国会議員 (member of the Diet; Diet member; member of parliament) + や (and) + 総理大臣 (prime minister (as the head of a cabinet government)) + も (too; also; as well) + 「君」 ("kun") + を (indicates the direct object of action) + つけて (て-form of つける (to attach; to join; to add; to append; to affix; to stick) which is used to connect to the next verb 呼びます) + 呼びます (to call; to address)]

岸田文雄君とか安倍晋三君 Kishida Fumio-kun, Abe Shinzou-kun, and so on [岸田文雄君 (Kishida Fumio-kun) + とか (and the like; such as; among other things; and so on) + 安倍晋三

Vocabulary Continued

君 (Abe Shinzou-kun)]

と言った具合です for example [と言った (like; such as ~) + 具合 (way; manner) + です (be; is)]

どうして why; for what reason

君をつけるのでしょうか why do (we) attach "kun"? [君 (kun) + を (indicates the direct object of action) + つける (to attach; to join; to add; to append; to affix; to stick) + のでしょうか (ask a question in a polite way)]

これは it; this [これ (it; this) + は (adds emphasis)]

明治時代 Meiji period (1868-1912)

江戸時代の末期に end of the Edo Period (1603-1868) [江戸時代 (Edo period (1603-1868)) + の (of; modifier) + 末期 (closing years (period, days); last stage; end stage) + に (specifies time)]

さかのぼります to go back (to the past or origin); to date back (to); to trace back (to)

吉田松陰という人が始めた「松下村塾」で at the "Shoukasonjuku" which was started by a man named Yoshida Shouin [吉田松陰 (Yoshida Shouin) + という (named; called) + 人 (person; someone) + が (identifies who performs the action) + 始めた (started; plain past form of 始める (to start; to begin)) + 「松下村塾」 ("Shoukason-juku"; a private school) + で (at; indicates the location of action)]

たくさんの若者たちが勉強していました many young men were studying [たくさん (many; plenty; a large number) + の (modifier) + 若者たち (young men; young people; youth; たち is a pluralizing suffix (especially for people and animals)) + が (identifies who performs the action) + 勉強していました (were studying; ていました-form of 勉強する (to study) which places focus on the duration of a past action)]

が but; however

身分によって depending on status [身分 ((social) standing; status; position; rank) + によって

Vocabulary Continued

(depending on; according to; how to use: Noun + によって)]

名前の呼び方が違いました the way (their) names were called varied [名前 (name; given name) + の (modifier) + 呼び方 (way of calling) + が (emphasizes the preceding word) + 違いました (varied; polite past form of 違う (to vary; to differ))]

相手が武士なら if the other person is a samurai [相手 (other person) + が (emphasizes the preceding word) + 武士 (samurai; warrior) + なら (if; in case; if it is the case that)]

「佐々木様はどう思われますか？」 "What do you think, Sasaki-sama?" [「」 (quotation marks; " ") + 佐々木様 (Sasaki-sama; 様 (Mr.; Mrs.; Miss; Ms.; honorific or respectful (*sonkeigo*) language, after a person's name (or position, etc.))) + は (indicates the sentence topic) + どう思われますか (what do (you) think?; どう (how; in what way; how about) + 思われます (polite passive positive form of 思う (to think)) + か (question marker))]

「佐々木様はどう思われますか？」という呼び方になりますし (they) would say, "What do you think, Sasaki-sama?", and [「佐々木様はどう思われますか？」 ("What do you think, Sasaki-sama?") + という (that; is used to define, describe, and generally just talk about the thing itself) + 呼び方 (way of calling) + になります (come to; turn out to; become) + し (and; and what's more)]

相手が農民なら if the other person is a farmer [相手 (other person) + が (emphasizes the preceding word) + 農民 (farmer; peasant) + なら (if; in case; if it is the case that)]

「佐々木殿の意見を聞きたい。」 "(We) would like to hear your opinion, Sasaki-dono." [「」 (quotation marks; " ") + 佐々木殿 (Sasaki-dono; 殿 (Mr.; Mrs.; Miss; Ms.; indication of respect to a person or a title; form of address used for official letters and business letters, and in letters to inferiors)) + の ('s; of; modification) + 意見 (opinion; view; comment) + を (indicates the

Vocabulary Continued

direct object of action) + 聞き^きたい (like to hear; from 聞く^き (to hear; to ask; to listen); ~たい means "want to do something"; a verb suffix that adds a meaning of desire; how to use: Verb (ます-stem form) + たい)]

「佐々木殿の意見を聞きたい。」となります would be "(We) would like to hear your opinion, Sasaki-dono." [「佐々木殿^{さ さ き どの}の意見^{いけん}を聞^ききたい。」("(We) would like to hear your opinion, Sasaki-dono.") + と (quotation marker; used for quoting (thoughts, speech, etc.)) + なります (to get; to become; to turn out)]

身分によって呼び方が違うのはよくないと that it is not good to address differently according to status [身分^{みぶん} ((social) standing; status; position; rank) + によって (according to; depending on) + 呼^よび方^{かた} (way of calling) + が (emphasizes the preceding word) + 違^{ちが}う (to vary; to be different) + の (nominalizer; turns the preceding clause into a noun phrase) + は (indicates the sentence topic) + よくない (not good; plain negative form of よい (good; excellent; fine; nice; pleasant)) + と (that; used for quoting (thoughts, speech, etc.))]

すべての生徒に「君」を付けて呼ぶことを勧めました (Yoshida Shouin) recommended that all students be addressed with "kun" [すべて (all; the whole; everything) + の (of; modifier) + 生徒^{せいと} (student; pupil) + に (to; into) + 「君」^{くん} ("kun") + を (indicates the direct object of action) + 付^つけて (て-form of 付^つける (to attach; to join; to add; to append; to affix; to stick) which is used to connect to the next verb 呼ぶ) + 呼^よぶこと (be addressed; 呼^よぶ (to call; to address) + こと ((must) do; how to form: Verb (dictionary form) + こと)) + 勧^{すす}めました (recommended; polite past form of 勧^{すす}める (to recommend (someone to do); to advise; to encourage; to urge))]

相手の身分に関係なく regardless of the other person's status [相手^{あいて} (other person) + の ('s; of; modifier) + 身分^{みぶん} ((social) standing; status; position; rank) + に関係^{かんけい}なく (regardless of ~; how to use: Noun + に関係^{かんけい}なく)]

Vocabulary Continued

相手を尊重して respect others [相手 (others; other person) + を (indicates the direct object of action) + 尊重して (て-form of 尊重する (to respect) which is used to connect to the next phrase)]

話ができる can talk [話 (talk; conversation) + が (is used with potential form of a verb) + できる (can; to be able to do; plain potential form of する (to do))]

からです is because [から (because; since) + です (be; is)]

これが this [これ (this) + が (emphasizes the preceding word)]

国会でも even in the Diet [国会 (National Diet; legislative assembly of Japan (1947-)) + でも (even)]

取り上げられて is taken up, and [て-form of 取り上げられる (plain passive positive form of 取り上げる (to take up; to adopt)) which is used to connect to the next phrase, creating the meaning of "and"]

今でも続く習慣になりました became a custom that still continues to this day [今 (present; in now; this day) + でも (still; yet) + 続く (to continue; to last; to go on) + 習慣 (custom; practice) + になりました (became; polite past form of になる (become; come to; turn out))]

ANIME / MANGA PHRASE
Surprise your Japanese friends with these phrases

Please see the sound files for the pronunciation

「 私 の 友だちは、・・・ 私 が 決めます。」

古味硝子のセリフ

アニメ「古味さんはコミュ症です」より

"As for my friends, ... I decide."
Line of Komi Shouko
From the anime "Komi Can't Communicate"

VOCABULARY

「」 —(quotation marks; " ")

私の友だち my friend [私 (I; me) + の ('s; indicates possessive) + 友だち (friend; companion)]

は wa—as for (indicates the sentence topic)

私が決めます I decide [私 (I; me) + が (identifies who performs the action) + 決めます (to decide; to choose; to determine)]

Vocabulary Continued

古味硝子のセリフ　line of Komi Shouko [古味硝子 (こみしょうこ) (Komi Shouko) + の (of; 's; modifier) + セリフ (one's lines; speech; words)]

アニメ　anime; animation; animated film; animated cartoon

「古味さんはコミュ症です」　"Komi Can't Communicate" [「」 (quotation marks; " ") + 古味 (こみ) (Komi) + さん (is an honorific suffix which means Mr., Mrs., or Miss that can be used with both first and last names and both genders) + は (indicates the sentence topic) + コミュ (communication) + 症 (しょう) (illness) + です (be; is)]

より　from

Kobayashi Issa 小林一茶
こばやしいっさ

あきかぜ
秋風や　むしりたがりし

あか　はな
赤い花

Haiku Audio

Autumn breeze | wanted to pluck | red flower

Explanation:

Explanation

（意味）秋風がふいています。この赤い花を（死んだ）あの子はむしりたがっていたなぁ。

（解説）小林一茶が亡くなった娘を思って作った俳句と言われています。赤い花は、おそらく彼岸花でしょう。幼い娘が欲しがった花を眺めながら、

17

Continued

<ruby>娘<rt>むすめ</rt></ruby> の<ruby>生<rt>い</rt></ruby>きていた<ruby>頃<rt>ころ</rt></ruby>を<ruby>思<rt>おも</rt></ruby>い<ruby>出<rt>だ</rt></ruby>しているという<ruby>切<rt>せつ</rt></ruby>ない<ruby>俳句<rt>はいく</rt></ruby>です。

(Meaning) The autumn wind is blowing. This red flower is a flower that the girl (who died) wanted to pluck.

(Explanation) It is said that Kobayashi Issa wrote this haiku thinking of his dead daughter. The red flowers are probably higanbana (red spider lily). The haiku is a poignant reminder of the time when his daughter was alive, while gazing at the flowers that his young daughter wanted.

Vocabulary

秋風 autumn breeze; fall breeze [秋 (あき) (autumn; fall) + 風 (かぜ) (wind; breeze)]

や (emphasizes the preceding word) [it's a *kireji* (cutting word) which indicates a pause, both rhythmically and grammatically, and may add an emotional flavor to the word/phrase preceding it]

むしりたがりし wanted to pluck [expresses the past tense form of むしりたがる (want to pluck; from むしる (to pluck; to pick);〜がる means "wants to do 〜 (third person)"; how to form: Verb (たい form) たい + がる)]

赤い花 red flower [赤い (あか) (red; crimson; scarlet) + 花 (はな) (flower)]

小林一茶 Kobayashi Issa (1763 – 1828) [A Japanese poet and lay Buddhist priest. He is

Vocabulary Continued

known as simply Issa, a pen name which means "Cup-of-tea". He is regarded as one of the four Haiku masters in Japan.]

意味 meaning; significance; sense

秋風がふいています the autumn wind is blowing [秋風 (autumn wind; fall breeze) + が (identifies what performs the action; emphasizes the preceding word) + ふいています (is blowing; ています-form of ふく (to blow (of the wind)) which is used to describe a continuous action)]

この赤い花を（死んだ）あの子はむしりたがっていた this red flower is a flower that the girl (who died) wanted to pluck [この (this) + 赤い花 (red flower) + を (indicates the direct object of action) + 死んだ (died; plain past form of 死ぬ (to die; to pass away)) + あの (that; the) + 子 (child; kid) + は (indicates the sentence topic) + むしりたがっていた (wanted to pluck; from むしる (to pluck; to pick); 〜たがっていた is the ていた form of 〜たがる (wants to do 〜 (third person)) which places focus on the duration of a past action)]

なぁ (casual suffix) [is used when you express your opinion or feeling]

解説 explanation; commentary

小林一茶が Kobayashi Issa [小林一茶 (Kobayashi Issa) + が (identifies who performs the action; emphasizes the preceding word)]

亡くなった娘を思って作った俳句 wrote the haiku thinking of (his) dead daughter [亡くなった (passed away; plain past form of 亡くなる (to die; to pass away)) + 娘 (daughter) + を (indicates the direct object of action) + 思って (て-form of 思う (to think)

Vocabulary Continued

which is used to connect to the next phrase) + 作った (wrote; plain past form of 作る (to make; to write)) + 俳句 (haiku; 17-mora poem)]

と言われています (it) is said that [と (that) + 言われています (is said; ています-form of 言われる (plain passive positive form of 言う (to say)) which describes a continuous action; how to form: Verb て-form + います)]

おそらく probably; (most) likely

彼岸花 higanbana; red spider lily (Lycoris radiata); cluster amaryllis

でしょう it seems; I think; I guess; I wonder

幼い娘が very young daughter [幼い (very young; little) + 娘 (daughter) + が (identifies who performs the action; emphasizes the preceding word)]

欲しがった花を眺めながら while gazing at the flowers that (his young daughter) wanted [欲しがった (wanted; from 欲しい (wanting; desiring; wishing for); plain past form of 欲しがる (want; desire; ~がる is used to describe how other people seem to feel, based on how they look or behave; how to form: drop the final ~い of an い-adjective and add ~がる)) + 花 (flower) + を (indicates the direct object of action) + 眺めながら (while gazing at; from 眺める (to look at; to gaze at); ~ながら means "while; as; during"; how to form: Verb (ます-stem form) + ながら)]

娘の生きていた頃を思い出している (he) remembers the time when (his) daughter was alive [

Vocabulary Continued

娘 (daughter) + の (modifier) + 生きていた (was alive; ていた-form of 生きる (to live; to exist) which places focus on the duration of a past action; how to form: Verb て-form + いた) + 頃 (when; around; about; how to form: Verb (casual) + 頃) + を (indicates the direct object of action) + 思い出している (remember; ている-form of 思い出す (to recall; to remember; to recollect) which is used to describe the actual state or condition of the subject; how to form: Verb て-form + いる)]

という that; called [is used to define, describe, and generally just talk about the thing itself]

切ない俳句 heartrending haiku [切ない (painful; heartrending; trying) + 俳句 (haiku)]

です be; is

LEVEL **BEGINNER**
JLPT N5

JLPT N5 Kanji

On: **カ**

Kun: **ひ**

Meaning: fire

Hint: Think of it as sparks coming from a person.

Audio of Readings

The left then right sparks are written first.

Stroke Order:

火 ヽ 丶 ⺌ 火

Examples:

はなび
花火 fireworks [note how the *hi* becomes a *bi*]

ひばな
火花 sparks [sometimes you can reverse kanji and get a different meaning—note here how the *hana* becomes *bana*]

Audio of Example

かざん
火山 volcano [lit. fire mountain]

かようび
火曜日 Tuesday

かようび
あしたは火曜日です。

Tomorrow is Tuesday.

VOCABULARY:

あした tomorrow

は (indicates the sentence topic)

火曜日 Tuesday

です be; is

22

～中

ABOUT:

中 by itself means "inside" or "in." However, when attached to a noun, it adds the meaning of "during" or "while" or "throughout." It is either pronounced as ちゅう or じゅう. There appears to be no set rule for when to use either pronunciation. Learn a few examples by heart.

HOW TO USE:

■ Add to nouns or phrases to indicate duration or coverage.

EXAMPLES:

[throughout]

彼は、一日<u>中</u>、テレビを見ました。

He watched TV **all** day long.

[he-as for-throughout the day-TV-(direct object marker)-saw]

Example 1

[during]

仕事<u>中</u>なので、彼は外に出られません。

He is work**ing**, therefore he cannot leave.

[work-during-therefore-he-outside-cannot leave]

Example 2

23

Continued

[during a future time]

^{らいしゅうちゅう} ^{しゅくだい}
来週中に、宿題をすませましょう。

Sometime **in** the next week, let's finish the homework.

[next week-during-homework-let's finish]

Example 3

VOCABULARY:

彼　he; him

は　(indicates the sentence topic)

一日中　all day long; all the day; throughout the day [一 (one; 1) + 日 (day) + 中 (throughout)]

テレビ　television; TV

を　(indicates the direct object of action)

見ました　saw [polite past form of 見る (to see; to look; to watch; to view)]

仕事中　at work; in the midst of work; working [仕事 (work; job; labor) + 中 (during)]

なので　because of; given that; since; therefore; so [how to use: Noun + な + ので]

Vocabulary Continued

外に　outside [外 (outside; exterior) + に (to; expresses direction)]

出られません　cannot leave [polite potential negative form of 出る (to leave; to exit; to go out; to come out)]

来週中に　sometime in the next week; within the next week; during the next week [来週 (next week) + 中 (during a future time; within) + に (specifies time)]

宿題　homework; assignment

すませましょう　let's finish [polite volitional form of すませる (to finish; to make an end of; to get through with; to let end); volitional form is used when making a suggestion to one or more people including oneself]

よんでみよう！ LET'S READ!

Learn through reading for (very) beginners of Japanese

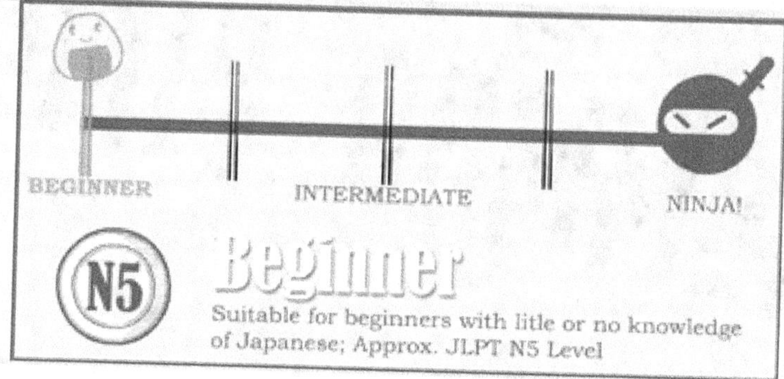

Have you only recently learned hiragana but need practice? Or perhaps, your hiragana is no problem, but you want to build your reading comprehension?

This segment is here to the rescue!

Read real Japanese—beginner level but not boring Japanese! Enjoy reading flash fiction, super short essays, and funny stories of common mistakes made by foreigners in Japan.

Best of all, the only requirement is that you can read hiragana. Vocabulary and grammar will be defined and explained.

The format is a little different from our other more advanced readers. The idea is for the reader to read the entire story three times. Each page will have a sentence or two in hiragana (with spaces between words for you to see "words" instead of syllables) at the top and that same content in full Japanese (with furigana) at the bottom. The middle will have the glossary and grammatical explanations. Lastly, the story will be presented in Japanese without furigana. See if you can read it after going through the explanations.

If you have just learned hiragana, you may want to listen to the sound file while reading the hiragana section to practice correct pronunciation. If you have studied Japanese a bit longer, you may want to start with the bottom version and take note of the glossary for understanding.

Makoto+ members can access this in a more interactive format. To learn more: **http://MakotoPlus.com**

And now...

Let's learn about...

DISASTER PREPAREDNESS DAY

Normal Speed

Slow Speed

Normal Speed

Slow Speed

防災の日

DISASTER PREPAREDNESS DAY

く　がつ　ついたち　は「ぼうさい　の　ひ」です。ぼうさい　の　ひ　は、じしん　や　おおあめ　など　の　ために　ように　を　する　ひ　です。

GLOSSARY AND NOTES

9月1日 *ku gatsu tsuitachi*—September 1 [9月 (September; 月 (month)) + 1日 (1st day of the month; 日 (day (of the month)))]

は *wa*—(indicates the sentence topic)

「防災の日」 *「bousai no hi」* —"Disaster Preparedness Day" [「」 (quotation marks; " ") + 防災 (disaster preparedness; prevention of damage resulting from a natural disaster; protection against disaster) + の (of; modifier) + 日 (day)]

です *desu*—be; is

地震や大雨などのために *jishin ya ooame nado no tame ni*—for earthquakes, heavy rain, etc. [地震 (earthquake) + や (such things as …; and … and) + 大雨 (heavy rain) + など (et cetera; etc.; and the like; and so forth) + のために (for)]

用意をする日です *youi o suru hi desu*—is a day to prepare [用意をする (get ready; prepare) + 日 (day) + です (be; is)]

9月1日は「防災の日」です。防災の日は、地震や大雨などのために用意をする日です。

この ひ は、いろいろな ばしょ で じしん が おこった とき
の ため の くんれん が おこなわれます。せんきゅうひゃくに
じゅうさん ねん（たいしょう じゅうに ねん）く がつ ついたち
に かんとう だいしんさい が おこりました。

GLOSSARY AND NOTES

この日は *kono hi wa*—this day [この (this) + 日 (day) + は (indicates the sentence topic)]

いろいろな場所で *iroirona basho de*—in various places [いろいろな (various; all sorts of; variety of) + 場所 (place; location; spot) + で (at; in; indicates the location of action)]

地震が起こったときのための訓練が行われます *jishin ga okotta toki no tame no kunren ga okonawaremasu*—drills are held to prepare for earthquakes; drills are conducted for the time when earthquake occurred [地震 (earthquake) + が (indicates the subject of the verb) + 起こった (occurred; plain past form of 起こる (to occur; to happen)) + とき (time; moment) + のための (for;「Noun-A + のための + Noun-B」means that Noun-B is for the benefit of Noun-A) + 訓練 (training; drill; practice) + が (identifies what performs the action; emphasizes the preceding word) + 行われます (is/are held; polite passive positive form of 行う (hold; conduct; perform))]

1923年（大正12年）9月1日に *sen kyuu hyaku ni juu san nen (taishou juu ni nen) ku gatsu tsuitachi ni*—on September 1, 1923 (Taishou 12) [1923年 (1923; 年 (year)) + 大正12年 (Taishou 12; 大正 (Taishou)) + 9月1日 (September 1) + に (on; specifies time)]

関東大震災が起こりました *kantou daishinsai ga okorimashita*—the Great Kanto earthquake occurred [関東 (Kantou; region consisting of Tokyo and surrounding prefectures) + 大震災 (great earthquake (disaster)) + が (identifies what performs the action; emphasizes the preceding word) + 起こりました (occurred; polite past form of 起こる (to occur; to happen))]

この日は、いろいろな場所で地震が起こったときのための訓練が行われます。１９２３年（大正１２年）9月1日に関東大震災が起こりました。

この　ひ　を　わすれない　よう　に　と　いう　いみ　で、く　がつ
ついたち　が　「ぼうさい　の　ひ」に　なりました。にほん　は、じ
しん　や　たいふう　など　さいがい　の　おおい　くに　です。

GLOSSARY AND NOTES

この日を忘れないように *kono hi o wasurenai you ni*—to remember this day; so that (you) won't forget this day [この　(this) + 日　(day) + を　(indicates the direct object of action) + 忘れないよう に　(so that ... won't forget; 忘れない　(don't forget; plain negative form of 忘れる　(to forget)) + よ うに　(so that ~; in order to); how to form: Verb（ない-form) + ように)]

という意味で *to iu imi de*—mean; that means [という　(that) + 意味　(meaning; significance; sense) + で　(て-form of です　(be; is) which is used to connect to the next phrase)]

9月1日が「防災の日」になりました *ku gatsu tsuitachi ga*　「*bousai no hi*」*ni narimashi- ta*—September 1 became the "Disaster Preparedness Day" [9月1日　(September 1) + が (emphasizes the preceding word) + 「防災の日」　("Disaster Preparedness Day") + になりました (became; polite past form of になる　(become; turn out; come to))]

日本は *nihon wa*—Japan [日本　(Japan) + は　(indicates the sentence topic)]

地震や台風など *jishin ya taifuu nado*—such as earthquakes and typhoons [地震　(earthquake) + や (such things as ...; and) + 台風　(typhoon; hurricane) + など　(et cetera; etc.; and the like; and so forth)]

災害の多い国です *saigai no ooi kuni desu*—is a country prone to disasters [災害　(calamity; disas- ter) + の　(of; modifier) + 多い　(frequent; common; a lot; many; prone) + 国　(country; state) + で す　(be; is)]

この日を忘れないようにという意味で、9月1日が「防災の日」
になりました。日本は、地震や台風など災害の多い国です。

29

ひごろ　から　じゅんび　を　して　おきましょう。

GLOSSARY AND NOTES

日ごろから　*higoro kara*—on a regular basis; on a daily basis; on a routine basis [日ごろ (normally; habitually) + から (from; by; on)]

準備をしておきましょう　*junbi o shite okimashou*—be prepared; let's get ready in advance [from 準備をする (get ready; make preparations); 〜ておきましょう is the polite volitional form of 〜ておく (to do something in advance; how to form: Verb て-form + おく); volitional form is used when making a suggestion to one or more people including oneself]

日ごろから準備をしておきましょう。

防災の日

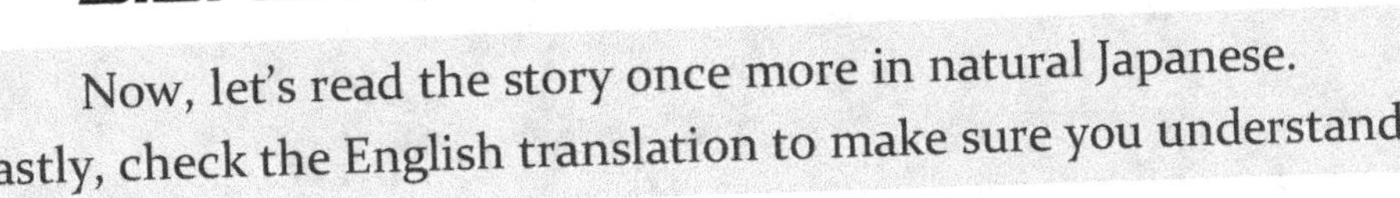

Normal Speed

Slow Speed

9月1日は「防災の日」です。防災の日は、地震や大雨などのために用意をする日です。この日は、いろいろな場所で地震が起こったときのための訓練が行われます。1923年（大正12年）9月1日に関東大震災が起こりました。この日を忘れないようにという意味で、9月1日が「防災の日」になりました。日本は、地震や台風など災害の多い国です。日ごろから準備をしておきましょう。

ENGLISH: (try to save this for last)

September 1 is "Disaster Preparedness Day". Disaster Preparedness Day is a day to prepare for earthquakes and heavy rain. On this day, drills are held in various places to prepare for earthquakes. 1923 (Taishou 12), on September 1, the Great Kanto earthquake occurred. September 1 was designated as "Disaster Preparedness Day" to remember this day. Japan is a country prone to disasters such as earthquakes and typhoons. Be prepared on a daily basis.

KEY VOCABULARY

9月1日 *ku gatsu tsuitachi*—September 1 [9月 (September) + 1日 (1st day of the month)]

関東大震災 *kantou daishinsai*—Great Kanto earthquake of 1923

防災の日 *bousai no hi*—Disaster Preparedness Day

地震 *jishin*—earthquake

大雨 *ooame*—heavy rain

台風 *taifuu*—typhoon; hurricane

災害 *saigai*—calamity; disaster

訓練 *kunren*—training; drill; practice

日ごろ *higoro*—normally; habitually

準備をしておきましょう *junbi o shite okimashou*—be prepared; let's get ready in advance

用意をする *youi o suru*—get ready; prepare

31

JAPANESE READER

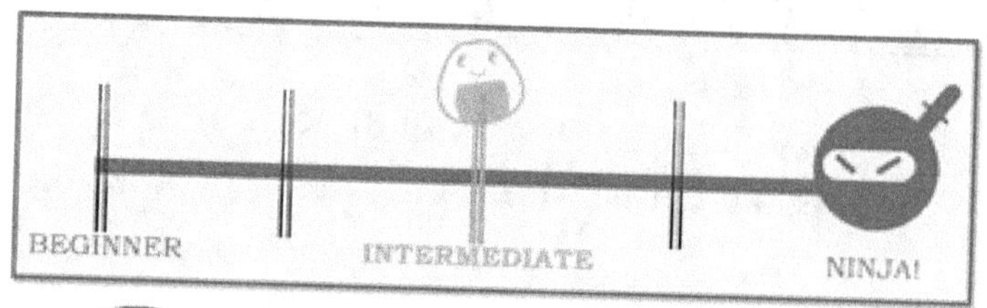

てづかおさむ

手塚治虫

Tezuka Osamu

手塚治虫 in 1951

Story Read Normal

Story Read Slow Speed

Work through the story, sentence-by-sentence, referring to the vocabulary and grammar explanations below as needed.

漫画の神様と呼ばれた人がいます。「手塚治虫」です。本名は、手塚治なのですが、虫が大好きなので、自分の名前の一番最後に虫をつけました。

漫画の神様と呼ばれた人 a man who has been called the god of manga [漫画 (manga; cartoon; comic; comic strip) + の (of; modifier) + 神様 (god; God) + と呼ばれた (has been called; was known; was referred; plain passive positive past form of と呼ぶ (to call; to refer)) + 人 (person; someone; somebody)]

(が)います there is/are (living things) [Noun + (が)いる]

「手塚治虫」です he is "手塚治虫" [「手塚治虫」("Tezuka Osamu"; 「」 (quotation marks; " ")) + です (be; is)]

本名は (his) real name [本名 (real name) + は (indicates the sentence topic)]

手塚治なのです is 手塚治 [手塚治 (Tezuka Osamu) + なのです (shows emphasis; how to use: Noun + な + のです)]

が but; however

虫が大好きなので because he loves insects [虫 (insect; bug; cricket; moth) + が (indicates the object of emotion) + 大好き (liking very much; loving (something or someone); adoring; being very fond of) + なので (because of; since; given that; how to use: な-adjective + な + ので)]

自分の名前の一番最後に to the end of (his) name [自分 (myself; yourself; oneself; himself; herself) + の ('s; of; indicates possessive) + 名前 (name; given name) + の (of; modifier) + 一番 (most; number one) + 最後 (end; last) + に (to)]

虫をつけました added 虫 [虫 (*mushi*; insect; bug; cricket; moth) + を (indicates the direct object of action) + つけました (added; polite past form of つける (to attach; to join; to add; to append; to affix; to stick))]

さて、この人は一体何をしたのでしょうか？彼は、

１９２８年（昭和３年）に大阪で生まれました。小学生

のころから、漫画を描きはじめ、

さて well; now; then

この人は this man [この (this) + 人 (man; person; people) + は (indicates the sentence topic)]

一体 exactly; precisely; ever; just; at all

何をしたのでしょうか what did (this man) do [何 (what) + を (indicates the direct object of action) + した (did; plain past form of する (to do)) + のでしょうか (ask a question in a polite way)]

彼は he [彼 (he; him) + は (indicates the sentence topic)]

1928年(昭和3年)に in 1928 (Shouwa 3) [年 (year) + 昭和3年 (Shouwa 3) + に (in (specifies time))]

大阪で生まれました was born in Osaka [大阪 (Osaka (city, prefecture)) + で (in; indicates the location of action) + 生まれました (was born; polite past form of 生まれる (to be born))]

小学生のころから when (he) was in elementary school; since (he) was an elementary school student; from grade-schooler [小学生 (elementary school student; primary school student; grade school student; grade-schooler) + のころ (when; around; about; how to use: Noun + の + ころ) + から (from; since)]

漫画を描きはじめ he started drawing cartoons, and [漫画 (cartoon; comic; comic strip; manga) + を (indicates the direct object of action) + 描きはじめ (started drawing and; ます-stem form of 描きはじめる (to start to draw; how to form: Verb (ます-stem form) + はじめる) which is used to connect to the next phrase, creating the meaning of "and")]

生徒たちはもちろん、学校の先生にも人気のある漫画を描いていました。そして、つらい戦争を経験しました。戦争が終わると、どんどん漫画を描き始め、プロとしてデビューしました。

生徒たちはもちろん学校の先生にも among students and school teachers alike; not only students but also among the school teachers [生徒たち (students; たち is a pluralizing suffix (especially for people and animals)) + はもちろん (not only ... but also ~; not to mention; let alone; of course; naturally; how to use: Noun + はもちろん + 2nd clause + も) + 学校 (school) + の (of; modifier) + 先生 (teacher; instructor; master) + にも (also; as well; too; alike)]

人気のある漫画を描いていました (he) was drawing popular manga [人気のある (popular; an adjectival clause that describes the next word 漫画) + 漫画 (cartoon; comic; comic strip; manga) + を (indicates the direct object of action) + 描いていました (was drawing; ていました form of 描く (to draw; to paint) which places focus on the duration of a past action)]

そして then; and; and then

つらい戦争を経験しました experienced a painful war [つらい (painful; bitter; heart-breaking; difficult (emotionally)) + 戦争 (war) + を (indicates the direct object of action) + 経験しました (experienced; polite past form of 経験する (have an experience; to undergo))]

戦争が終わると after the war; when the war ended [戦争 (war) + が (identifies what performs the action; emphasizes the preceding word) + 終わる (to end; to finish; to close) + と (if; when; is used to express successive actions, which is a chain of actions where one is immediately followed by another; emphasizes the immediacy)]

どんどん more and more; increasingly; rapidly

漫画を描き始めプロとしてデビューしました (he) began drawing cartoons and debuted as a professional [漫画 (manga; cartoon; comic; comic strip) + を (indicates the direct object of action) + 描き始め (began drawing and; ます-stem form of 描き始める (to begin to draw; how to form: Verb (ます-stem form) + 始める) which is used to connect to the next phrase, creating the meaning of "and") + プロ (professional) + として (as (i.e. in the role of)) + デビューしました (debuted; polite past form of デビューする (debut; come out; make a debut appearance))]

手塚治虫の漫画は、たいへんな人気となりますが、この人は漫画を描いただけではありません。日本で初めてテレビアニメを制作しました。「鉄腕アトム」は、１９６３年にテレビで放送されました。

手塚治虫の漫画 Tezuka Osamu's comic art [手塚治虫 (Tezuka Osamu) + の ('s; of; indicates possessive) + 漫画 (cartoon; comic; comic art; manga)]

たいへんな人気となります become extremely popular [たいへんな (extremely; very; greatly) + 人気 (popularity; public favor) + となります (become; turns into certain state; having reached to its final state)]

が but; however

この人 this person [この (this) + 人 (person; people; someone)]

漫画を描いただけではありません (he) did more than just draw cartoons [漫画 (manga; cartoon; comic) + を (indicates the direct object of action) + 描いた (drew; plain past form of 描く (to draw; to paint; to sketch)) + だけ (only; just; merely; simple) + ではありません (is/are not)]

日本で in Japan [日本 (Japan) + で (in; indicates the location of action)]

初めてテレビアニメを制作しました produced the first TV animation [初めて (first; first time) + テレビ (television; TV) + アニメ (animation; animated film; animated cartoon; anime) + を (indicates the direct object of action) + 制作しました (produced; polite past form of 制作する (to produce; to create; to make))]

「鉄腕アトム」 "Astro Boy" [「」 (quotation marks; " ") + 鉄腕アトム (Astro Boy)]

1963年に in 1963 [年 (year) + に (in; specifies time)]

テレビで放送されました was broadcasted on TV [テレビ (TV; television) + で (on; indicates the location of action) + 放送されました (was broadcasted; polite passive positive past form of 放送する (to air; to broadcast; to transmit))]

大変な人気となり、4年間放送されました。アトムの顔や絵が描かれたおもちゃやお菓子がたくさん売れました。それをきっかけに、ほかの人たちもアニメをつくるようになり、日本はアニメでいっぱいになりました。

大変な人気となり4年間放送されました became very popular and was broadcasted for four years [大変な (very; greatly) + 人気 (popularity; public favor) + となり (became and; ます-stem form of となる (to become; turns into certain state; having reached to its final state) which is used to connect to the next phrase, creating the meaning of "and") + 4年間 (four years; 年間 (period of a year)) + 放送されました (was broadcasted)]

アトムの顔や絵が描かれたおもちゃやお菓子が toys and snacks which have a picture and face of Astro Boy drawn on them [アトム (Astro Boy) + の ('s; of; modifier) + 顔 (face) + や (and) + 絵 (picture; drawing; painting; sketch) + が (identifies what performs the action; emphasizes the preceding word) + 描かれた (drawn; plain passive positive past form of 描く (to draw; to paint; to sketch)) + おもちゃ (toy) + お菓子 (snacks; confections; sweets; candy; cake)]

たくさん a lot; lots; plenty; many; a large number; much

売れました sold; was/were sold [polite past form of 売れる (to sell (well))]

それをきっかけに this started; this led; take this opportunity [それ (that; it) + を (indicates the direct object of action) + きっかけに (taking advantage of; with ... as a start; inspired by)]

ほかの人たちも other people also [ほか (other (place, thing, person)) + の (of; modifier) + 人たち (people; たち is a pluralizing suffix (especially for people and animals)) + も (too; also; as well)]

アニメをつくるようになり to start making animated cartoons, and [アニメ (animation; animated film; animated cartoon; anime) + を (indicates the direct object of action) + つくる (to make; to produce) + ようになり (ます-stem form of ようになる (to start to; to come to point that; to become able to) which is used to connect to the next phrase, creating the meaning of "and")]

日本はアニメでいっぱいになりました Japan became full of anime [日本 (Japan) + は (indicates the sentence topic) + アニメ (anime; animation; animated cartoon) + で (of) + いっぱい (full; filled (with)) + になりました (became; polite past form of になる (become; come to; turn out to))]

鉄腕アトムなどのアニメは、日本だけでなく、外国でも放送さ

れるようになりました。今、日本はもちろん、世界中でアニメ

が大人気となっていますが、

鉄腕アトムなどのアニメ animations such as Astro Boy
[鉄腕アトム (Astro Boy) + など (et cetera; etc.; and the like; and so forth) + の (of; modifier) + アニメ (anime; animation)]

日本だけでなく、外国でも not only in Japan but also in other countries [日本 (Japan) + だけでなく (not only ... but also ~; how to use: Noun + だけでなく) + 外国 (foreign country; other countries) + でも (also; as well)]

放送されるようになりました came to the point that (it) was broadcasted [放送される (plain passive positive form of 放送する (to air; to broadcast; to transmit)) + ようになりました (polite past form of ようになる (to start to; to come to point that; to become able to))]

今 today

日本はもちろん、世界中で not only in Japan but around the world [日本 (Japan) + はもちろん (not only; let alone; how to use: Noun + はもちろん) + 世界中 (around the world; throughout the world) + で (in; indicates the place where an action occurs)]

アニメが大人気となっています anime has become very popular [アニメ (anime; animation; animated film; animated cartoon) + が (emphasizes the preceding word) + 大人気 (very popular; highly favoured) + となっています (has become; ています-form of となる (turns into certain state; having reached to its final state) which is used to describe the actual state or condition of the subject; how to form: Verb て-form + います)]

が and

この日本のアニメを生み出したのが手塚治虫だったのです。

彼の代表作は、「ジャングル大帝」「リボンの騎士」「火の鳥」や「ブラックジャック」などがあります。

この日本のアニメを生み出したのが the one who cre-ated this Japanese anime [この (this) + 日本 (Japan) + の (of; 's; modifier) + アニメ (anime; animation; animated film; animated cartoon) + を (indicates the direct object of action) + 生み出した (created; polite past form of 生み出す (to create; to bring forth; to produce)) + の (one; placeholder for nouns like 事 (non-physical thing) or 物 (material thing)) + が (emphasizes the preceding word)]

手塚治虫だったのです was Tezuka Osamu [手塚治虫 (Tezuka Osamu) + だった (was; were; plain past form of です (be; is)) + のです (shows emphasis)]

彼の代表作 his masterpiece [彼 (he; him) + の ('s; indicates possessive) + 代表作 (most important work (of a writer, artist, etc.); representative work; masterpiece)]

「ジャングル大帝」「リボンの騎士」「火の鳥」や「ブラックジャック」など "Jungle Emperor," "Princess Knight," "Phoenix," "Black Jack," etc. [「ジャングル大帝」 ("Jungle Emperor") + 「リボンの騎士」 ("Princess Knight") + 「火の鳥」 ("Phoenix") + や (such things as ...; and ... and) + 「ブラックジャック」 ("Black Jack") + など (et cetera; etc.; and the like; and so forth); 「や…など」 contains the meaning "there are other similar things"]

(が)あります there is/are (non-living things)

ここには書ききれないくらいの数の作品があり、どれも人気が

ありました。子供向けだけでなく、大人のための作品も作りま

した。

ここには here [ここ (here) + には (puts more emphasis and restriction on the preceding word)]

書ききれないくらいの数の作品があり there are too many works to the extent that (I) can't write them all, and; there are too many to list, and [書ききれない (can't write; from 書く (to write; to list; to compose); ~きれない means "unable to do; too much to finish"; how to form: Verb (ます-stem form) + きれない) + くらい (approximately; about; around; to the extent ~) + の (modifier) + 数 (quantity) + 作品 (work (e.g. book, film, composition, etc.); opus; performance) + (が)あり (there are; ます-stem form of 「(が)ある」 (there is/ are) which is used to connect to the next phrase, creating the meaning of "and")]

どれも any; all; every

人気がありました was/were popular [polite past form of

人気がある (popular; be liked by everybody; star; enjoy popularity; be well thought of)]

子供向けだけでなく大人のための作品も作りました (he) created works not only for children but also for adults [子供 (child) + 向け (intended for …; oriented towards …; aimed at …) + だけでなく (not only… but also ~) + 大人 (adult; grown-up) + のための (for; for the benefit of; how to use: Noun-A + のための + Noun-B) + 作品 (work (e.g. book, film, composition, etc.)) + も (too; also; as well) + 作りました (created; polite past form of 作る (to create; to make))]

彼は 働 きすぎで、寝る時間は毎日３時間ほどしかなかったそう

です。徹夜もよくしたそうです。彼は、がんのため、６０歳で

亡くなりましたが、

彼 he; him

働きすぎで work too hard, and; working too much,

and [働きすぎ (from 働く (to work; to labor); indicates the act of working too much; is a noun that
refers to a specific state (working too much); ~すぎ
is the stem form of すぎる (to be excessive; to be
too much; to be too …) which functions as a noun;
how to form: Verb (stem form) + すぎ) + で (て-
form of です (be; is) which is used to connect to the
next phrase, creating the meaning of "and")]

寝る時間 time for sleeping; sleepy time; time for sleep;
time for bed [寝る (to sleep (lying down)) + 時間
(time)]

毎日3時間ほどしかなかった (he slept) only about
three hours every day [毎日 (every day) + 3時間
(three hours; 時間 (hour)) + ほど (about; around;
approximately; or so) + しかなかった (was only;
plain past form of しかない (only; nothing but; how
to form: しか + Verb (ない form)))]

そうです people say that; it is said that; I hear that

徹夜もよくしたそうです it is said that (he) often
stayed up all night [徹夜 (staying up all night) + も
(emphasizes the preceding word) + よく (often;
frequently) + した (did; plain past form of する (to
do)) + そうです (people say that; it is said that; I
hear that)]

彼は、がんのため he (died) of cancer; he (died) because of cancer [彼 (he) + は (indicates the sentence topic) + がん (cancer) + のため (of; because
of)]

60歳で亡くなりました (he) died at the age of 60 [60
歳 (60 years old; 歳 (-years-old; age)) + で (at) +
亡くなりました (died; polite past form of 亡くなる
(to die; to pass away))]

が but; however

病院のベッドでも鉛筆を握って仕事を続けようとしたそうで
す。一生の間、１７万枚の漫画を描き、７００以上の物語を
作り上げた手塚治虫。

病院のベッドでも even in (his) hospital bed [病院 (hospital; clinic) + の ('s; of; modifier) + ベッド (bed) + でも (even)]

鉛筆を握って仕事を続けようとした (he) held a pencil and tried to keep working [鉛筆 (pencil) + を (indicates the direct object of action) + 握って (held and; て-form of 握る (to hold; to clasp; to grip) which is used to connect to the next phrase, creating the meaning of "and") + 仕事 (work; job; labor) + 続けようとした (tried to keep on; from 続ける (to continue; to keep up; to keep on); 「Verb (volitional form) + とした」 means "tried to do")]

一生の間 during (his) lifetime [一生 (whole life; a lifetime; all through life; one existence) + の (of; modifier) + 間 (period of time (during, while); duration)]

17万枚の漫画を描き draw 170,000 manga and [17万 (170,000; 万 (ten thousand)) + 枚 (counter for flat objects (e.g. sheets of paper)) + の (of; modifier) + 漫画 (manga; cartoon; comic; comic strip) + を (indicates the direct object of action) + 描き (draw and; ます-stem form of 描く (to draw; to paint; to sketch) which is used to connect to the next phrase, creating the meaning of "and")]

700以上の物語を作り上げた created more than 700 stories [700 以上 (more than 700; 以上 (more than; above)) + の (of; modifier) + 物語 (story; tale; narrative) + を (indicates the direct object of action) + 作り上げた (created; plain past form of 作り上げる (to create; to put together; to build up; to complete))]

天国で、今も漫画を描き続けているような気がしています。

天国で in heaven [天国 (paradise; heaven) + で (in; indicates the location of action)]

今も漫画を描き続けている (he) is still drawing manga today; has been drawing manga even now [今も (still; even now; 今 (now; present time) + も (even)) + 漫画 (manga; cartoon) + を (indicates the direct object of action) + 描き続けている (has been drawing; ている-form of 描き続ける (continue drawing; from 描く (to draw; to paint; to sketch); how to form: Verb (stem form) + 続ける) which is used to describe an ongoing action; how to form: Verb て-form + いる)]

ような気がしています (I) feel as if [ています-form of ような気がする (feel as if; feels like; have a feeling that; seems like; how to use: Verb (casual) + ような + 気がする;「気がする」 is used when you sense something) which is used to describe the actual state or condition of the subject; how to form: Verb て-form + います]

Tezuka Osamu

Please try to tackle the Japanese first and use this only as needed.

There is a man who has been called the god of manga. He is "手塚治虫 (Tezuka Osamu)".

His real name is 手塚治, but he added "虫 (insect)" to the end of his name because he loved insects. Now, what exactly did this man do?

He was born in Osaka in 1928 (Shouwa 3). He started drawing cartoons when he was in elementary school, and his cartoons were popular among students and school teachers alike. Then, he experienced the painful war. After the war, he began drawing more and more cartoons and debuted as a professional. Tezuka Osamu's comic art became extremely popular, but he did more than just draw cartoons.

He produced the first TV animation in Japan. "Astro Boy" was broadcasted on TV in 1963. It became very popular and was broadcasted for four years. Many toys and snacks with Astro Boy's face and picture on them were sold. This led other people also to start making animated cartoons, and Japan became full of them. Animations such as Astro Boy were broadcasted not only in Japan but also in other countries.

Today, anime is very popular not only in Japan but around the world, and the one who started all this anime was Tezuka Osamu. His masterpieces include "Jungle Emperor," "Princess Knight," "Phoenix," and "Black Jack." There are too many to list here, and they were all popular. He created works not only for children but also for adults.

He worked too hard and it is said he slept only about three hours every day. He often stayed up all night. He died of cancer at the age of 60, but even in his hospital bed, he held a pencil and tried to keep working. During his lifetime, Tezuka Osamu drew 170,000 manga and created more than 700 stories.

I feel as if he is still drawing manga in heaven today.

手塚治虫

　漫画の神様と呼ばれた人がいます。「手塚治虫」です。本名は、手塚治なのですが、虫が大好きなので、自分の名前の一番最後に虫をつけました。さて、この人は一体何をしたのでしょうか？

　彼は、1928年（昭和3年）に大阪で生まれました。小学生のころから、漫画を描きはじめ、生徒たちはもちろん、学校の先生にも人気のある漫画を描いていました。そして、つらい戦争を経験しました。戦争が終わると、どんどん漫画を描き始め、プロとしてデビューしました。手塚治虫の漫画は、たいへんな人気となりますが、この人は漫画を描いただけではありません。

　日本で初めてテレビアニメを制作しました。「鉄腕アトム」は、1963年にテレビで放送されました。大変な人気となり、4年間放送されました。アトムの顔や絵が描かれたおもちゃやお菓子がたくさん売れました。それをきっかけに、ほかの人たちもアニメをつくるようになり、日本はアニメでいっぱいになりました。鉄腕アトムなどのアニメは、日本だけでなく、外国でも放送されるようになりました。

　今、日本はもちろん、世界中でアニメが大人気となっていますが、この日本のアニメを生み出したのが手塚治虫だったのです。彼の代表作は、「ジャングル大帝」「リボンの騎士」「火の鳥」や「ブラックジャック」などがあります。ここには書ききれないくらいの数の作品があり、どれも人気がありました。子供向けだけでなく、大人のための作品も作りました。

　彼は働きすぎで、寝る時間は毎日3時間ほどしかなかったそうです。徹夜もよくしたそうです。彼は、がんのため、60歳で亡くなりましたが、病院のベッドでも鉛筆を握って仕事を続けようとしたそうです。一生の間、17万枚の漫画を描き、700以上の物語を作り上げた手塚治虫。

　天国で、今も漫画を描き続けているような気がしています。

Kanji in Focus

It is usually helpful to create a story based on the meanings of the kanji parts. Often, different kanji learning systems will use different "meanings" for the parts. We try to give the most common ones, but consistency is best. Choose one meaning per kanji part and stick with it. The following are a selection of the kanji found in this story. The <u>underlined</u> reading is probably the most used.

漫	READINGS / MEANING / EXAMPLE	<u>マン</u>・みだりに・そぞろ cartoon; involuntarily; unrestrained; corrupt 漫画 (まんが) cartoon; comic; comic strip	氵 water 日 sun; day 罒 net 又 again; once again; crossed legs Allow *unrestrained* **water** 氵 under the **sun** 日 to flow in the **net** 罒 filters **once again** 又.
徒	READINGS / MEANING / EXAMPLE	<u>ト</u>・いたずら・あだ on foot; junior; emptiness; vanity; people 生徒 (せいと) pupil; student; schoolchild	彳 step; stop; linger; loiter 走 run; race *People* can't just **stop** 彳 the **race** 走.
戦	READINGS / MEANING / EXAMPLE	<u>セン</u>・いくさ・<u>たたか</u>う・おののく・そよぐ・わななく war; battle; match 戦争 (せんそう) war	⌣ small 田 field; rice field 十 ten 戈 halberd; arms; weapon; spear A **small** ⌣ *battle* **field** 田 for **ten** 十 warriors with **spear** 戈 and shield.
験	READINGS / MEANING / EXAMPLE	<u>ケン</u>・ゲン・あかし・しるし・ためす・ためし verification; effect; testing 経験 (けいけん) experience	馬 horse 僉 risk; all; together This **horse** 馬 underwent **all** 僉 the *verification* processes.
菓	READINGS / MEANING / EXAMPLE	カ candy; cake; fruit お菓子 (かし) snacks; sweets; candy; confections	艹 grass; herb; plant 田 field; rice field 木 tree; shrub; bush Decorate a *cake* with fresh flowers and **plants** 艹 of a **field** 田 surrounded by **trees** 木.

Kanji in Focus Continued

Kanji		Readings / Meaning / Example	Components & Mnemonic
寝	**READINGS** **MEANING** **EXAMPLE**	シン・ねる・ねかす lie down; sleep; rest 寝る to lie down; to sleep; to go to bed	宀 roof; house 爿 split wood; turtle 彐 broom; hands 冖 crown; cover 又 again; crossed legs A **roof** 宀 made of **split wood** 爿 and **broom** 彐, **covers** 冖 the man who is taking a *rest* while sitting on **crossed legs** 又.
徹	**READINGS** **MEANING** **EXAMPLE**	テツ sit up (all night); penetrate; clear; pierce 徹夜 staying up all night	彳 step; stop; linger; loiter 亠 lid 厶 private; elbow 月 moon; month 攵 strike; hit; folding chair *Clear* **steps** 彳 on how to set up the **lid** 亠 and **elbow** 厶 connector before this **month** 月 ends to **hit** 攵 the installation target.
間	**READINGS** **MEANING** **EXAMPLE**	カン・ケン・あいだ・ま・あい interval; space 時間 time; hour	門 gate 日 sun; day Measure the *interval* of **gate** 門 voltage within this **day** 日.
鉛	**READINGS** **MEANING** **EXAMPLE**	エン・なまり lead 鉛筆 pencil	金 gold ハ eight; legs 口 mouth; opening They search for high grade *lead*, **gold** 金 and **eight** ハ other types of metal from the **opening** 口 of the mountain.
握	**READINGS** **MEANING** **EXAMPLE**	アク・にぎる grip; hold; mould sushi; bribe 握る to hold; to clasp; to grasp; to grip	扌 hand 尸 flag 至 arrive; proceed; reach; attain Let's *hold* each other's **hand** 扌 while looking at our national **flag** 尸 flying high to **reach** 至 the sky.

MAKOTO

Do you have any questions? Anything confusing? Feel free to email me (Clay) at clay@thejapanshop.com with any questions, comments, or suggestions.

Do you have ideas to make *Makoto* better? We'd love to hear from you. Did something particularly help you? Love to hear that as well.

What to experience even more Makoto? Learn about our new Makoto+ membership. Download the latest issue or access web-based back issues. All this and more starting at only $3. Go to: **www.MakotoPlus.com** now!

Clay & Yumi